THE SIXTY S

Also by Rob Parsons

Loving Against the Odds

The Sixty Minute Father

The Sixty Minute Marriage

The Sixty Second Father

Rob Parsons

Hodder & Stoughton

LONDON   SYDNEY   AUCKLAND

ACKNOWLEDGEMENTS

With special thanks to Jonathan Booth, Sheron Rice and Elizabeth and Paul McCusker.

Copyright © Rob Parsons, 1997

First published in Great Britain in 1997

The right of Rob Parsons to be identified as the Author of this compilation has been asserted by him in accordance with the Copyright, Designs and Patents Act 1988.

1 3 5 7 9 10 8 6 4 2

British Library Cataloguing in Publication Data
A record for this book is available from the British Library

ISBN 0 340 69421 1

Typeset by Palimpsest Book Production Limited,
Polmont, Stirlingshire
Printed and bound in Great Britain by
Mackays of Chatham PLC, Chatham, Kent

Hodder and Stoughton
A division of Hodder Headline PLC
338 Euston Road
London NW1 3BH

To Arthur and Margaret Tovey

Somebody has said, 'The problem with fatherhood is that just about the time you're experienced – you're redundant!' For most of us the task is like going back to school.

These are some of the lessons I am learning as I go – some are for toddlers, others for teens, but most will affect every child.

Where the quotes are from notables, I've mentioned them, but most are from ordinary fathers who, like us, have learnt them the hard way.

*L*isten, I can be President of the United States, or I can control Alice. I cannot possibly do both.

President Theodore Roosevelt of his oldest daughter

*T*he skill of a surgeon, the cunning of a lawyer, the diplomacy of an ambassador, the insight of a scholar, the heart of a priest . . . this is what it takes to be a good father. Any takers?

*G*et involved with your newborn baby as much as possible. Change as many nappies as you can, and hold her in your arms often. Talk to her as if she can understand every word. Football will do fine.

*I*n fatherhood, timing is everything: knowing when to speak and when to listen, knowing when to act and when to be still, knowing when to correct and when to comfort, knowing when to lead and when to follow. Get the timing right and your children will hold you in awe – as will the rest of the world.

*I*t does not surprise me at all that few people claim fatherhood for themselves. The pains are too obvious, the joys too hidden.

Henri M. J. Nouwen

A girl's father is the first man in her life, and probably the most influential. Absent or involved, loving or rejecting, what he is, or was, leaves a lasting imprint.

David Jeremiah

I remember imagining that the egg-timer held not sand but the days of our children's lives. The first eighteen years contain 6,570 days. If your daughter is ten years old, you have 2,920 left. So far as is possible, in this busy world, try not to miss one of them.

When she was small, my daughter loved to have me read to her at bedtime. Just as we were getting to the most exciting part of the story, the phone would often ring. 'I'll only be a moment,' I'd say. One call led to another, but eventually I would remember that we hadn't got the frog back into a prince yet, and I'd rush back upstairs. But little eyes had fought to stay awake as long as they could.

*G*ather ye rose-buds while ye may,
  Old Time is still a-flying:
And this same flower that smiles today,
  Tomorrow will be dying.

              Robert Herrick

*P*arenting is not for cowards.

Dr James Dobson

*I*f we are going to make a difference as fathers, we need to do it *now*. The decision is practical. It has to do with bedtimes, Saturday football games, stories and hamburgers; and it has to do with carving those times out of busy lives – today.

'When we've finished decorating.'

'When I get promotion.'

'When I pass the examinations.'

Don't keep saying, 'Later,' to those you love. A slower day is coming, but you'll be too old to enjoy it.

*T*his is my library, and this the chair
My father used to sit in carelessly
After his soldier fashion, while I stood
Between his knees to question him.

Robert Browning

When my son, Lloyd, was small and I beat him at a game, I used to make him promise to tell nobody. He would nod his head solemnly and then run off shouting, 'I beat Dad! I beat Dad!'

*G*randmothers don't have to do anything except be there. When they read to us, they don't skip pages, or mind if it's the same story over and over again. Everybody should have a grandmother, especially if you don't have television – because they're the only grown-ups who have time.

Nine-year-old girl

*K*neel to talk to toddlers and listen with your eyes.

A small boy shouted downstairs, 'I'm scared of the dark.' His father yelled back, 'Don't be scared, God is with you.' There was silence for a moment and then, 'Get up here fast – I need somebody with skin on!'

*I*t's not just our jobs that keep us from our children – we say 'Yes' to almost anybody who asks us to do anything. We love to be busy; we want to be wanted. But those of us who say 'Yes' to the world end up saying 'No' to those who are closest to us and who need us most.

*I*recently spoke to someone who said, 'In our office, we dare not go home at six even if all the work is done. There's an unwritten rule that you hang around until eight and go home looking weary.'

I remember once speaking to five young men. I'd spent three hours advising them on a strategy to help them build their business. When I finished, I asked, 'Are any of you married with children?' They all were. I said, 'My great fear for you is that in ten years you'll be even wealtheir than you are now, but you will have lived those years as paupers.'

No one was ever heard to say on their deathbed, 'I wish I had spent more time at the office.'

I'd like my sons to think of me as I think of my father –
as a man whose stories were always worth hearing . . . a
man whose wisdom was always available, a man whose love
could always be relied on.

Anthony Astrachan

*W*e shouldn't have unreasonable expectations. One distraught father reported to a psychologist that his four-year-old was not yet reading. 'Obviously a case of low intelligence,' the expert commented. 'Really?' the father asked worriedly. 'Yes,' said the psychologist, 'Yours!'

Your child will forget the television you bought for his bedroom. It is true that it will seem kind to him. It will never say, 'Later.' And it will, in the isolation of his room, go about its business of educating him. But he will never forget the night that you and he slept in an old tent. And when he is old he will still remember it.

I turned to bribery via magnificent and thoroughly unsuitable gifts: a shining bicycle when he was too young to use it . . . when he wanted to play baseball, a set of gloves and masks and bats and uniforms that the Yankees would have envied. I confess it. I gave him everything but myself.

Edward G. Robinson

We weren't typical actor's kids. We were never part of the Hollywood jet set. My father's home life was very important to him. When he came home after a day at the studio, he wanted to relax, and that meant not talking about his work.

Jonathan, son of Gregory Peck

*I*f you are fortunate enough to have a job, do it with all your heart. But remember that although it is a vital part of your life, the day will come when somebody will take your place. Nobody will *ever* take your place as the father of the child you are now cradling in your arms.

Said to a father on the birth of his first child

*F*athers who have to be away from home a great deal have an especially hard task. One father in this situation said, 'When you have to be away from home, you must work harder at relationships. I let my children know in a dozen ways I'd rather be with them. And when I'm home, I let *nothing* rob me of that time with them.'

*C*hildren love receiving letters. If you have to be away from home, drop them a line.

*T*he sobering fact is that many of us have the ability to create unnecessary business. It doesn't matter whether the demands of the job are great or small, or even if we have a job at all; we fill our lives with activity that robs us of time for the things that matter.

*D*on't criticise anybody else's children until your own are well into their nineties!

*L*et your children overhear you praising them to someone else.

*D*isplay your children's paintings on your desk or noticeboard at work and take them in to see them.

We are so busy giving our children what we didn't have that we don't have time to give them what we did have.

Dr James Dobson

*H*e was a good father, particularly to me. He loved me very tenderly, but he also loved pleasure.

Jean-Jacques Rousseau

When I'm gone and my children talk about me, I would love them to say that I had taught them great things ... But I would wonder if I had missed it if they didn't add, 'But what we remember, too, is that he was fun to be with.'

*D*raw funny faces on the bottom of each other's feet with washable felt-tips (it works best with young children!).

*A*cceptance doesn't mean that we don't motivate our children to do better. It doesn't even mean that we don't hope they'll change in some ways. It means that we don't put on them the burden of trying to be somebody they cannot be.

*K*atie has a whole life in front of her filled with those who will want her when she succeeds. I want to motivate her to be the best she can be. But more than that, I want her to know that my love for her is based not on success but on the fact that I'm her father.

A man recounted the time he had run home from school and told his father he had finished second in the whole county in his music exam. He said, 'My father asked, "Won't you ever come in first?"' The man continued, 'I am nearly fifty years of age. I am responsible for two hundred staff, I have four children of my own, and I am still trying to prove myself to my own father.'

A woman wrote to me, 'I was a disappointment to my father. He wanted a son. He never hugged me, praised me, or told me he loved me. I have forgiven him, but my self-esteem is very low, I am often depressed, I am riddled with guilt; *I am eighty-five years old.*'

*W*e want our children to achieve, but more than that we want them to be successful as people. For that they need a sense of security, and there is no greater security than knowing that even if my sister is cleverer, tidier, and better at sports, I am loved *anyway*.

*S*ince my daughter Katie was twelve, we've gone on 'dates' together. It might be a cup of coffee, a pizza or just a walk. Those evenings have been a lifesaver for us. Away from the interruptions of home, they have been 'adult' times, which Katie has felt were special. We've often sat with a coke for an hour or more and just talked.

When I crashed the car the first person I called was my Dad. I didn't need him to tell me how silly I'd been, or how expensive it would be to repair. I needed him to say that it would be all right, that I wasn't as useless as I felt, and that he still loved me.

Susan, aged seventeen

*S*aying 'I love you' should be done sparingly. Like breathing.

*C*an't you understand? I never wanted your place or your money. I don't want to hold anything. All I wanted was a father, not a boss. I wanted you to love me.

Richard Brooks

*H*e that will have his son have a respect for him and his orders must himself have a great reverence for his son.

John Locke

*E*very child needs someone who is irrationally positive about them.

Guy Dowd

*T*he power of praise is awesome. There is hardly a person on the face of the earth who does not respond to it. Most of us know how effective it can be in the work situation but forget that, to a child, it can be like rain in the desert.

Never under-estimate the power of touch. A hand placed on your child's shoulder, a caress of her hair, a quick squeeze of the hand, an embrace . . . these small gestures will stay with your children long after more 'profound' expressions have faded from memory.

*F*athers, do not exasperate your children, in case they lose heart.

Colossians 3:21

*I*f someone praises your child to you – be sure to tell him what was said.

*T*he secret of being a good father? Water balloons. A wild water balloon fight will break down all barriers, all resentments, all disagreements. Only make sure Mum doesn't catch you doing it in the living room.

*S*urprise your children. Be glad when you hear them tell their friends, 'I think my father may be crazy.'

*A*cknowledge when your children are toddlers that you're out to ruin their lives. That will rob them of half their complaints when they're teenagers!

*T*he element which was chiefly deficient in his moral relation to his children was that of tenderness. I do not believe that this deficiency lay in his own nature. I believe him to have had much more feeling than he habitually showed, and much greater capacities of feeling than were ever developed.

John Stuart Mill, of his father

When playing games with small children, let them win occasionally! Don't play monopoly with a four-year-old as if your life depended on winning.

*W*hether it's setting a tea table for a collection of stuffed animals, building cities out of mud, or playing a game you've played a hundred times . . . try this exercise: let your child teach *you* how to do it.

*S*o-called 'quality time' is an expression made up by busy parents, not children. The problem with communicating with children is that often you have to put in a lot of quantity time so that the quality can really happen.

Start a hobby or leisure activity with your child that is not dependent on physical fitness. You may do it together for the rest of your life.

*P*ass on to your children the most significant lesson you learned from your father or an older person you knew as a child.

If we listen to them when they are five, six, or seven, there's a chance they'll listen to us when they are fifteen, sixteen, and seventeen.

*R*ules without relationship lead to rebellion.

Josh McDowell

When I was a boy of fourteen, my father was so ignorant I could hardly stand to have the old man around. But when I got to be twenty-one, I was astonished at how much he had learned in seven years.

Mark Twain

*W*hen a teenager says, 'I have to go with my parents,' and makes it sound like chewing garlic for breakfast, he probably means, 'They care enough about me to want me with them.'

David Jeremiah

*I*f you burden him with many rules, one of these two things must necessarily follow; that either he must be very often punish'd ... or else you must let the transgressions of some of your rules go unpunish'd ... and your authority become cheap to him. Make but few laws, but see they be well observ'd when once made.

John Locke

*T*he time will come when your children will test the boundaries you have set. It is practically a sacred moment. There is nothing so destined to breed insecurity in a child than his believing that there are no rules and, even if there are, nobody cares if he breaks them.

*L*ook for situations in which you can praise your children. *Catch them doing something right.*

I have decided there is only one way to get revenge on your teenagers for the dreadful things they put you through: grow old and be a burden to them.

Parent of three teenagers

*D*on't be upset if your teenagers are embarrassed to be seen out with you. They'll let you take the bag off your head long enough for you to pay for the jeans.

Now that I'm a teenager, my parents don't hug me. But when no one's looking, I wish they still would.

Boy of fourteen

A father will do well, as his son grows up . . . to talk familiarly with him . . . ask his advice, and consult with him about those things wherein he has any knowledge or understanding. By this, the father will gain two things . . . The one is, that it will put serious considerations into his son's thoughts, better than any rules or advices he can give him . . . Another thing . . . will be his friendship.

John Locke

*A*sk your teenager these three questions:
What irritates you the most about me?

What do you like most about me?

What would you like to see improved or changed in our relationship?

The joys of parents are secret; and so are their griefs and fears.

Francis Bacon

*M*y children have reached that age when they're too embarrassed to be seen with me. I just wish they'd get to that age when they're too embarrassed to ask me for money.

*A*t his table he liked to have, as often as he could, some sensible friend or neighbor to converse with, and always took care to start some ingenious or useful topic for discourse, which might tend to improve the minds of his children. By this means he turned our attention to what was good, just, and prudent in the conduct of life.

Benjamin Franklin, of his father

*T*each your children how to handle money; help them prepare a simple income/expenditure budget and keep track of it.

*T*his is a caution not to treat your son with too much harshness and severity. Consider, he is but a boy, and that there was a time when you were so too. In exerting, therefore, the authority of a father, remember always that you are a man, and the parent of a man.

Pliny the Younger, to his son

*T*here have been times when you say you understand me. But you really don't. There have been times when I tell you about my problems in the hope of your advice or support. But quite often you shrug me off saying, 'That's nothing . . . you should have our problems.'

Letter from a teenager to his parents

*T*he fastest way to get my dad's attention was to do something wrong.

Woman in her twenties
looking back on her teenage years

*B*ut though direct moral teaching does much, indirect does more; and the effect my father produced on my character did not depend solely on what he said or did with that direct object, but also, and still more, on what manner of man he was.

John Stuart Mill

In other words, 'Values are more caught than taught.'

When your children leave home, write them a letter and tell them three things you want them to remember for ever.

To the Memory of My Father . . .

*T*he longer I live, the better I understand the kindness of
thy heart and

the high quality of thy mind.

The efforts which I have devoted to these studies, as well
as those which

preceded them, are the fruit of thy counsel and example.

Desiring to honour these filial rememberances, I dedicate
this work to thy memory.

Louis Pasteur

*N*ever give up on the relationship with your child, whatever age they are – even if they have left home under a cloud.

*T*he bad news is that we are still going to be worrying about these children when they are grown. A woman of ninety-five once came into my legal practice. She said, 'I can rest in peace now; I've just got my youngest son into an old people's home.' (*She* wasn't in one.)

*M*any a man has discovered a relationship with his father years after leaving home. But even at this stage of life, the same two ingredients are needed as when your children were small: time, and the courage to seize the day.

*B*ut while he was still a long way off his father saw him, and his heart went out to him; he ran to meet him, flung his arms round him, and kissed him . . . 'Let us celebrate with a feast. For this son of mine was dead and has come back to life; he was lost and is found.'

Luke 15:20–4

'**B**ut Dad said . . .'
Give your wife a break! Don't fall into the trap of letting your child play one parent off against the other – decide the rules between you and stick to them.

*T*rain them and trust them.

*D*on't read your child's school reports as though they are a prophecy of the future; there are some surprises in store – *both* ways!

*I*t is yours . . .
Although the print be little, the whole matter
And copy of the father; eye, nose, lip,
The trick of's frown, his forehead, nay, the valley,
The pretty dimples of his chin and cheek, his smiles,
The very mould and frame of hand, nail, finger . . .

Paulina to King Leontes of his new baby
in *A Winter's Tale* by William Shakespeare

*D*on't take all the credit; don't take all the blame.

When my children were small we would occasionally have what we called a 'family night'. We would all drag our mattresses downstairs and sleep on the family room floor together. There's no logical reason why four people with perfectly good beds should want to do that – except that it's fun.

*I*f you are able to pass on a financial gift to your children, do it when they are in their mid-thirties. They'll need it then.

Be kind to thy father, for when thou wert young,
Who loved thee so fondly as he?
He caught the first accents that fell from thy tongue,
And joined in thy innocent glee.

Margaret Courtney

*D*evelop family traditions. These could be as simple as cooking hamburgers every Saturday night – it helps give children roots and they will remember them when they are grown.

*P*ut dates in your diary that are important to your children: birthdays, school concerts, sports events.

*D*esperate to help her mother get to her father, who is very ill, Jo goes on a secret errand.

'That's my contribution . . .'

'My dear . . . Twenty five dollars! Jo! I hope you haven't done anything rash?'

'No . . . I only sold what was my own.'

As she spoke, Jo took off her bonnet, and a general outcry arose, for all her abundant hair was cut short.

Louisa M. Alcott

*B*egin compiling a family history with your child. Include the family tree, traditions, photographs, newspaper clippings, certificates and recipes.

*I*f possible take your child to your place of work. Let them sit or stand in your place. Tell them how you spend your day.

*W*hen your children are small read aloud to them by candlelight.

*I*n the little world in which children have their exist-ence, whosoever brings them up, there is nothing so finely perceived and so finely felt as injustice.

Charles Dickens

*T*ry not to slip into a lifestyle that means the family rarely eats together.

A children's doctor once advised that if you want to know why most children are scared of hospitals, just drop to your knees next time you're in one. From your young child's viewpoint, it's a different world.

*T*each your son also to love and fear God while he is yet young, that the fear of God may grow in him, and then God will be a husband to you, and a father to him: a husband and a father which cannot be taken from you.

Sir Walter Raleigh to his wife, on the eve of his death

On the first day of a new school term, the teacher used to send home a letter to every parent.

It read, 'If you promise not to believe all that your child tells you goes on at school, then I promise not to believe all they tell me goes on at home.'

Never assume that you know your children so well that they can't surprise you any more.

Next time you go to your child's school play, don't video it. Watch it.

*I*nsanity is hereditary; you get it from your children.

*W*hen your children are grown, don't insist they spend Christmas with you.

*W*hat we don't like in our children is often what we have most successfully passed on.

*L*iberty and indulgence can do no good to children . . . and on the contrary, imperiousness and severity is but an ill way of treating men . . . unless you have a mind to make your children, when grown up, weary of you, and secretly to say within themselves, When will you die, father?

John Locke

*C*hildren aren't necessarily better than other people. Like the child in 'The Emperor's New Clothes', they are just apt to be better at telling the difference between a put-up job and the real thing.

Frederick Buechner

Υou can con a con but you can't kid a kid.

Josh McDowell

S ometimes the only reason to try again is . . .
'for the sake of the children'.

*T*he greatest thing you parents can do for your children is to love each other.

Dr Benjamin Salk

A husband and wife that love and value one another, show their children . . . that they should do so too. Others visibly lose their authority in their families by their contempt of one another.

William Penn

*M*y dad doesn't love my mum any more and he's found somebody else. But he doesn't know how sad it's made us, 'cos if he did he would never have gone.

Boy, aged eight

*T*he life we mould will almost certainly one day step into those same parental shoes. And there's the great challenge: to be an effective father not just for the sake of our children, but for the sake of *their* children.

*H*e was a man, take him all in all, I shall not look upon his like again.

Hamlet of his father

I put my hand over hers and told her . . . quite seriously, not to get too attached to the little thing, because she couldn't keep him. I did this to try to spare her what I had seen happen to other women . . . who were nearly destroyed by the discovery that, purely and simply, children are crops. One raises them and they go away.

Preston Sturges, Sr, on the birth of his newborn son

One night, when my son Lloyd was small, I was saying prayers with him. The next day I was due to fly abroad to address an international law conference and I was quite nervous. I've prayed many prayers for him, but this time asked him to pray for me. This is what he said:

'Dear Lord, please help my dad to be brave, and not to make too many mistakes.' It's not a bad prayer for every father.